THE SWEATING JOKER POEMS

The Sweating Joker Poems

Written by

Stephen Philip Means

Wisdomgame®

Copyright 2012 by Stephen P. Means

All rights reserved. No part of this book may be used or reproduced in any manner whatsoever without written permission except in the case of brief quotations embodied in critical articles or reviews.

Published 2012

WISDOMGAME®

ISBN 978-0-9792448-8-9

Deep Appreciation

I want to thank Walt Hopmans for his continual open support to all poets and writers in Santa Barbara. Poetry is a special kind of communication. Keats wrote "A thing of beauty is a joy forever. Its loveliness increases; it will never pass into nothingness; but still will keep a bower quiet for us, and a sleep full of sweet dreams, and health, and quiet breathing." Walt, thank you for the many joys you have supplied to all of us.

The Sweating Joker

Silken sheen sequins glistening green pearl and red,
The sweating joker stepped on stage,
Reciting from an internal page
Smiled as he bled
And bared his balls and cried
"Would anyone care
If I died,
Or on a dare
If I juggled one or one hundred
Words in the air?"

But no one spoke
And no one laughed,
No one took a poke.
No guffaw and no one gaffed.
The sweating joker stood alone
In the condition of contention
Gnawing on that bone.

He bared his self
And like a little elf
He laughed and laughed insane
Until he jumped and balanced even higher
Tiptoeing back and forth upon the wire,
And poems burst from the juggler vain.

Peanut Butter Day

She creams, craves the crumbs of coffee cake.
What to order, ought to order
A clack of eggs, pancake on plate.

Sugar shocks her sinking soul,
But the coffee cup can't fill her up.
What to order? Ought to order.
She craves the crumbs of coffee cake.

Her counter offer issues
From the kitchen coffer.
No clack of eggs. No pancake on plate.
Give me peanut butter,
And make it straight.

But instead, with celerity,
She slaps it on some celery
And solves the morning munchies
With peanut butter crunchies.

If I Could Call a Cloud

If I could call a cloud
By naming perfection,
I would bend upon my knee
And call your name.

To see the bright light of your eyes
And the beauty of your smile,
It makes me laugh.
Oh, warm yellow morning sun,
But it's only you,
You are so beautiful.

Gorgeous.
Beyond comparison.
Images can not define
Nor names describe this seduction.

So I will not call clouds
Or bow to call your name,
And I will not name perfection.
I will not name perfection
Nor water down this seduction.

You are the fragrance of the flower.
The spray, the wave, the whistling breeze,
The air itself.
Bite by bite,
I eat your warm nectar.

Peddler's Choice

I scream ice cream
Down the hungry streets
Where dirt below, filth above
Is more want than love.

Ice cream? Ice cream?
It's fresh and pure from me;
Good and cheap, not free.
Tutti-fruity, chocolate, or cherry?

Ice cream? Ice cream?
Calling at my buyers
Brings me no lovers.
Rocky road, vanilla, or berry?

I scream, I scream
And cry and pound my chaste
But never melt the ice
That makes love last.

I scream ice screams
That pierce the day
And bring the bitter in
To take my sweets away.

Dialectic

Despised hatred, playfully working
Wrong to right, truthfully wronged.
Its cause et paramar neon, neon.
Trapie. Dingo tapie. Its salon.
We. Or. Is. Can't slagate. Can tank.
Jogging, forms, dringo, my mind
Can tank er us, the hold Oman shouts
I don't want to live anymore.

Beatific benefits clergy's clarification
Rectified baptismal, dismal youth
Personified in holy sheets,
Compute the infinite Aleph Null:
More fully stated, sea is empty,
Still, moving, dripping soul.
I don't want to live anymore.

Balanced systemic polemic Platonic
Truthfully wronged . . . hatefully despised
Sealed intuition, candied idea, bitter wet
All breath, forced outside, inside, out to
I don't want to live anymore.

The Princess

The Princess De De Fat,
The unmarried American Empress
Ordered
For her fourth pregnancy
A pizzaburger and a cola.
It was miscarried
By bad delivery
And she had to settle
For pancake and pastrami on rye,
Giving her gas
Making her talk
Of naming the baby
Chew De Fat.

Flash Back

I dug my channeled machine.
So long it looked, and mean
As I slid behind the wheel
Revved it, and started to squeal
Into one lane and out again.
Was it safe to snort cocaine?

I turned the music up so loud,
Leaned back, slouched and proud,
Then my buddy had to shout. Alarm!
About tracks running up his arm
About us being busted
And how we should rip,
How my rod should be dusted
Right on down to the strip.

The Edge of Time

I was walking on East Beach
And the crusty land beneath my toes
Crunched like meringue.
Was I the first person on the new morning sand?

The smiling sea's phosphorus suds
Appeared to joke at me
As I tiptoed along the laughing lotion.
I was a funny man, that morn,
Dawning on the sand.

The island's silhouettes were clear
Before the light blue sky.
I felt dear and clean.
A new man on new sand.

Between the bay
And the coveted Santa Barbara cove
Is an edge.
Strike a match in the dark and watch the flame.
It's that kind of boundary,
Flickering and undulating alive.
The pattern is never the same.

Nothing is ever the same.
Where the sand feels cool on the bottom of your feet
And the waves wash warmer over them,
Here is the edge of time.

Tonight

Oh moon, oh moon
The air cuts me like pin pricks
And I tremble, or could it be, I shiver.
The dark one rambles over desert floor.

Oh moon, so cold.
Oh moon, moon.
Pity the ill wind that blows its icy breath
And when touching my skin,
Will taste its own chilling death.

I am in a mood to catch ungodly things
And crack their shells
To rip and snarl and look
Directly into His shinning black opal eyes.

Moon, oh moon,
Protect me from myself.
Oh moon, protect me moon.
Protect me from myself.

Project your bright white light
In that brown and grey crevice
Between my silly yellow spineless self
And the me that lifts my eyes
My arms, my spirit, and shouts: Yes!

Moon. Moon. You are not a reflection.
You are your own light
Old and cold, you two are my only friends.
The jackal sleeps with me tonight.

Moon, oh moon,
Protect me moon.
Oh moon,
Protect me from myself.

Out on that deserted plain
I breathe in cold and breathe out warm
Clouds of lonely white blue air.
It seems it's only me, and Moon,
And stars in the sky everywhere.

Then behind, behind me on my back,
This presence, the eerie floating opalescent eyes
So silently, at last I turn and eat my locomotive heart
That's no longer beating in my chest
But straining the skin on my arms
The hair stands straight up
A void forms where I had a stomach
I am falling, falling.
Oh moon, oh moon, where is your light?
The jackal sleeps with me tonight.

He pulls my self into my arms
And I am entranced,
Those giant gleaming black and shinning eyes
Hold me, they hypnotize.
I feel the damp cold on my neck,
The steel shroud of sleep,
In pain, I realize
The moon sucks my soul with its light,
And the jackal sleeps with me tonight.

Debra

Her long fingers touching the back of my hand
And the fingernails up my arm,
The back of my neck flashed.
Hair stood up.
Her hands gripped my collar
Slid down my shirt and ripped it.
A button spun out in the air
Bouncing on the floor with a tinkling sound.
Her palms pressed my chest.
Her fingers swept over my stomach.
And caused me to swallow and burn.
Her tongue circled around
And her lips,
She sucked hard on my nipple.
Her dark hair smelled like almond,
Fresh, as I gripped the back of her head
Wrenched her face to mine
Her eyes, deep soft brown
Accepting and full of desire
Her mouth tasted like an exotic fruit
Alive and dripping succulent juices.
But her tongue, her tongue was a living lance of fire
An untamed twisting flame.
It shocked me and burned me and beckoned
And as it retuned she sucked my tongue deep into her
Until full in her mouth
It felt like she would pull it off the root.
From that moment on my voice was changed.
I could not say a word
Without her name coming before I spoke.
Debra, I need you.
Debra, I want you.
Debra.

Jill

Laying here nude on my bed

>The sheets turned down.
>The patchwork quilt refused
>And spurned by the wool blanket.
>The wool blanket itself rejected
>By the softness of the muslin.

My sex rests in the trough of my legs
Like a sullen sleepy monster,
A monster weary of chewing white fig blossoms
And of quelching red hot novas.

Remember the first time we made love . . .

The English countryside
The hedges and the roses
How the old woman who ran the inn
Demanded we tell her if we were married
But we couldn't lie . . .
And had to take separate rooms.

How you quietly opened the door
Your secret glance
My heart wildly beating
That fantastic down bed
The fragrance of Lilac and Rose
Our beautiful bodies, hot and moist.

Your lips are like that.
Your hair is the blonde mane of a wild mare.
You are white light
An angle, lifted on wing,
Who dances on the tips of her toes
And lifts her breasts,

                                        to sing.

HYKUS

Monkey Dance

Monkey dance Siamese cat climbs
Paws soft shoulder
Bites the ends of my hair.

Afternoon Clouds

Afternoon clouds bare darkness
Light breeze fluffs and lifts
Steam from one coffee cup.

Twilight Electric

Twilight electric lights shine
Evening comes steam rolling
Slowly over the city.

Jasmine

The fragrance of Jasmine reminds
Orange blossom remembers
Her perfume.

Fairies

Rain drops and the puddles dance
Crack flash. There are the fairies.
Here is the waiting.

The Most Dangerous Place

The most dangerous thing in the world is an open mike
At a poetry reading.
Because the people who are listening,
Aren't really listening.
They are getting ready to read their words,
Or they have just read their words
Or they are aptly listening for words so that they
Can say they heard so and so read
Or they are thinking about the big poetry feast
They had a few weeks ago and how
Later on they can throw up the whole thing
To their wives, or husbands, or dada or mama
And call it poetry.

They are simply thinking and not listening.

So this really is the most dangerous place in the world,
Because let's say you were out in big surf
Among the rocks and sharks
And the seaweed is dragging on your legs
And something splashes the water next to you
And a big set comes up and you get caught inside.
You had better hold your breath
And hold on to your surfboard
Or you'll be locked up with Davy Jones
For the next 400 years, dead as a doornail.

So there, in the water, you have to be alive, aware.
Here, in the ocean of words, sounds, and breath
You can sleep. You have nothing to fear here.
Words can't hurt you, can they?

Or, perhaps you should be awake and
Hold on to your chair.
Look out. Here comes a big one.

Antidisestablishmentarianism.

You make it over that one, then . . .
"Outside!" yells the scholar.
A big word. Building, swelling, rising up,
Getting ready to pound you.
You stroke for it. And the fear begins.
Will you make it over and be safe?
Or at the last minute, will you dig in,
Turn yourself around and stand like the King of Kings,
And ride that wave.

Self-retroflected-pyschoanalytical-
Multiphasic projection.
It comes crashing down on you like a ton of bricks.

But no!

You are up. You are standing. You walk the nose.
You hang five. You walk back. You dance on that word.

The crowd applauds.
Then you slip.

Muck, punk, slunk, junk
Slub, pub, mub, rub a dub
Bub de bub, de pubbles de bubbles
Puttes, poots, roots, toots,
Suits, snoots, hoots!
Pubbles de bubbles

You are buried by sounds.
Hold on to your chair. Hold your breath.
A poetry reading
With an open mike,
Is a most dangerous place to be.

Co-host

I live in a box.
They live below
To the side and on top of me.
They don't make any sound.
And neither do I.
They think I think
I think they think.
I meditate.
I go out.
I see them in the hallways
Looking at the floor
I come home.
We pass silently.
They sleep.

They think I sleep,
But I don't.

I tiptoe to their rooms.
I look at them,
Touch their clothes,
Sniff their breath.
I enter their dreams.

I am the symbol of their disgust.
My eyes bulge white without iris.
Rats cling to my chest.
Worms squirm from my nostrils.
The warm smell of decay follows me.
I make them dream lust.

Asylum

This paper is white. It's cold.
My voice breaks, crunches the crust, the ice.
I search through every word I've sung,
And then decide to write: Asylum.

The record is over, but my song didn't play.
They bring my white writing jacket
And cinch my hands behind my back.
Though short of breath, I manage to say: Asylum.

My eyes, I could see, were all that I'd need.
At least the bandage they taped over my mouth
Helped stifle the shock. I couldn't shout
As they pushed me about. I was able to read: Asylum.

Outside, in the cold, it all became clear.
To make sure I was dead . . . I know
They put a hood on my head and shoveled on snow.
Still, one word whispers inside of my head.

The End Table

Out in the garden in a old busted box
I found my collection of rocks,
Brown from the rust
Of a torn tin can where some old pennies hid.
The agates and mica were stained from the rust
And the polished stalactite had small little scratches.

There was Jasper, Obsidian and petrified wood . . .
I cleaned them all
And placed them on an end table
In the small entrance hall.
I picked a sweet smelling rose
From the bush Sharon had given me.
And placed it in front of the pennies and rocks
On top of the end table . . .

Deep in the kitchen I dug some buried sea salt
And put it in one of Mom's cut crystal cups
Which I placed in the front of them all,
In front of the pennies, the rose, and rocks
On the end table in the small entrance hall.

Bought at a thrift store, the old silver urn
Sounded a sharp ring as I thumped it.

Ting!

After dipping it in the pool
I held my hand over it
And made this prayer:
"Fill this space with compassion
May all who enter be blessed."
And flicked the water
Over them all
The pennies, rocks, salt and the rose
On the end table in the small entrance hall.

As I bent close
Wet pennies out of place.
Droplets seeping in the salt,
Rocks glistening,
The delicate scent of Rose.

Ding Dong Daddy

Ding Dong Daddy in your old blue jean
Ding Dong Daddy long and mean
Jump the fence and started to run
Got away from the wife to have some fun.

Went down to the bar to get a drink
Next thing you know his eyes are pink
Got so drunk he couldn't think
Went in the john and peed in the sink.

Got up on the stage and started to rage.
Played the guitar like rock and roll sage.
But the band and him weren't on the same page.
The police tossed the monkey into a cage.

Ding Dong Daddy woke up the next day
With a head ache that would not go away.
Had to call the wife.
To save his life.
To put up the bail
And get out of jail.

Oh Ding Dong Daddy in such a dream.
You're not so mean.
You and your big get away scheme;
You done tore a hole in your old blue jean.

The Chalice of Romance

The arroyo was dry and still,
The fall sun was warm.
For a moment the glare blinded me.
Or was it the laughter in your eyes
As we found a place, dusted the ground
And spread out the old Indian blanket.

From the wicker basket
I pulled out guavas, tangerines and oranges.
Could I juggle? Of course. Three at a time.
You laughed.
I sliced them with my knife and dripped
Them in my mouth and then in yours.

You held the wine glasses
While I poured the sangria.
Our glasses touched. Salute!
"Taste the blood of the Earth" I said.
You pulled me close.
I felt your breath on my face, my ear.
You whispered, "I want passion."

When we fell apart
In your eyes, I saw unquenchable fire
Feeding on itself,
Lusting for lust.

From the wicker basket
I lifted a red rose bud
And placed it gently in your empty glass.
"Passion," I replied, "Yes . . .
But passion burning in the chalice of romance."

Eucharist

I saw Jesus in the microwave
And Elvis in the air.
Buddha sang a song today,
But really they weren't there.
It was only me and mommy.
We were trying to forget.
We had nothing to eat.
We hadn't et yet.

Sonny . . . she called me sonny.
You know, it's not very funny.
You're such a slob.
You're not even a dude.
You ain't got no job.
Go get us some food!

I won't desist.
I must persist.
I'll boil my clothes.
Steam my dreams.
Cook all my faults.
Scramble my beliefs.
Make a list.
Microwave,
Eucharist!

My Bare Trees

I feel deciduous.
Someone has tuned a fork to my chrysalis
Shattering my dreams
Heaping my chaff in coruscating piles about my feet.

No. I'm mistaken.
These aren't diamonds.
They're embers.

My bare tree is burning itself inside out.

Gasoline fumes don't compare
To the sweet redolence of fresh burning flesh.
Neither knives nor shelves of barked skin
Can equal this torture of silence.

I am eating alive by myself.

Failure

Dreg damp sand seeps open my pores
And creeps the marrow blue
Up my legs to a brittle heart.
The land wants me back again.

Crunched, crushing tipped white
Transluce blue green phos suds
Crashing smashed empty wails
Echoes thuds.
The sea calls for me.

Fire's red fucus force growing
A thousand glowing yellow
Flickering orange flames
At it's head.
The daemon gnaws his teeth
And breathes on my neck,
Demanding crystal not wax.

Moiety

You, my dear diaphanous violet
Wrote Delacroix,
Are more sedate than dark sea blue,
Violent more than bloody rose.
And yet, somehow, I suppose
You hue is but a mixture of the two.

Oh gaudy, gaudy orange!
Yelled Seurat,
When he viewed the sun slowly set.
You're brighter than any mustard bloom,
And redder than any fowlish ploom.
And yet, and yet, he cried
Your hue is but a mixture of the two.

By riverside, beneath a tree, Cezanne sighed
And spoke of green serene.
It's true, he said, you are still part blue.
But oh you're so mellow for being part yellow.
It's true.
Your hue is but a mixture of the two.

Love's Jail Yard

Your honor . . .
I'll get down on my knees
I'll beg and I'll say
From the very first day
Right from the start
She stole my heart.

Judge hear my pleas
Down on my knees
I'll cry and I'll pine
And I'll wail
Give her a fine
Or send her to jail
Right from the start
She stole my heart

The jury will applaud
When she's proved a fraud
The case will unravel
So bring down the gavel
Today is the day
So please send her away
And please
Make her stay!

Right from the start
She broke my heart.

Down to the Pier

In spring the wind reaps clean the green racemes
And shakes a gossamer chrysalis to tremble, to dream
That the once green caterpillar worm wouldn't die
But transform into beauty, grows wings and fly.

As orange blossom fragrance scents the air
The feeling comes, a remembrance, something there.
A taste, a time forgotten, so long ago
When you were young, and you longed to grow;
When the sap ran strong and before it peaked
You loved lip to lip, and cheek to cheek.

In pastel gardens of your youth
Yellow orange red rose was the truth.
You jumped out of bed, awakened with the sun,
You played all day, the whole day was fun.
At night you prayed and wished upon a star,
But now, back in time,
In this springtime
You get a beer
Drive down on the pier
And sit in your car.

Practice

Somewhere, over there in the sky a bunch of colors
Are dancing, dancing in the mist
Making rainbows of violets, reds, and blues
And Dorothy is flying with golden slippers,
Toto at her heels,
Alice and the white rabbit at her side
Their mouths are open, speaking in tongue,
They are practicing poetry.

Somewhere, in a bed up high
Where fishes fly in the sky,
And black cats stare into each other eye,
A man and woman are curled like pretzels
Hot and sweating in each other's embrace.
Piston and cylinder, pumping like a well oiled motor,
They are practicing machine-gun-love.

The guru is deep within himself
And has become all that is now.
The images of his eternal self
Instantaneously become him.
Giant rhizomes fly out of the golden sun
And fall back in explosions of purple fizz.
He is practicing God.

She walks in beauty like the night.
Stands before the mirror.
Plumps her breasts.
Sleeks her hands down the ivory skin on her hips.
And with her hands on those hips all akimbo,
Pouts her lips, then shakes her head
No, no!
Pouts her lips again
Shakes a finger at the mirror.
No, no!
She is a practicing bitch.

The old man sits in a shed throwing out one of those
Como say yama?
Flipping devices that go out on a string
And come back to land in the cup.
Como say yama?
Flipping, flipping
But always missing.

From the corner of his eye, something distracts.
He turns. A close up of his face.
He's looking at you.
In slow motion the ball reaches the end of the string
And returns to land perfectly in the cup.

His eyes bulge in disbelief.
He stares at the ball and cup,
Grabs his chest.
His eyes curl back in his head.
Jerking and writhing he falls on the floor
He grabs his heart. Goodbye!

Close up of the white pasty face.
His eye lids flutter. He sits up. He's okay.
Just joking. He didn't die.
He was practicing.

Shadows Menace

My words bounce off the walls.
Food dry and stale.
High on a coffee rap
But no one's here to listen.

Shadows creep into the darkness.
Sounds where none belong.
Bed unmade. Desk cluttered.
Clothes need to be washed.

Paper towels scattered.
Last month's calendar.
Old tennis shoes.
Beach remnants.
Tangled hair.
Sound comes from nowhere.
Shadows menace.

Tommy

Bad brains blown bit by bit
America's children sit and squint
The channel-changer hell bent
Flicks scene after screaming scene
Just stops for an instant.
Marshall McLuhan proclaims
"The medium is the massage."
Tommy puts his face right up to the glass
Tightly twists the remote control.
Eyes toiling, brain boiling
Twelve, eighty, now five hundred
One thousand, ten thousand channels.
You're on line, you're connected man.
Forward, into the past
All images that have been
Will be, will forever last.
Edward R. Murrow says,
"TV, the vast wasteland,"
While Marilyn Manson sings The Who
"Tommy, Tommy, Tommy can you hear me?"
"Doom, let's play doom."

Bad brains blown bit by bit
I can't turn off my TV.
Tommy, can you hear me?

The Song of Tanya

Many years in the future a man volunteered to be rocketed deep into space. Every Saturday night we would listen for his report. At first, they were mathematical and difficult to understand, then a certain complacency set in and with it came an understandable depression. He was alone in the frozen cold of dark space, but he was brave and true, a poet. Finally, before he disappeared, the spaceman Tanya sang his report. Tanya was my hero. I follow in his footsteps, and I search for him. I search all of space for Tanya, but now I sing of him.

> I awoke cold and frozen stiff.
> Years I'd drifted in dreamless sleep,
> But now the central command had awakened me.
> It was my watch,
> That eerie hour each mate must walk the bridge
> To check the instrument
> And cast their electronic report into the ether
> To be received by whom
> To be heard by whom
> We know not.
> For space is warped
> And perhaps this suspended frozen animation
> Provides the means to return before our words
> For space and time is warped;
> Most probably when we do return
> Our words will sound to us as baby babble.
> As if a child could describe
> This darkness between the light.

> While the long bones of my fingers begin to thaw
> And the warm oxygen of the ship

Not unlike the real air of our blue planet
We once called . . .
I can not say the word
Without remembering sands that bark under feet.
Streams that gurgle secret language,
Lightening cracking fire falls into the sea
And volcanoes spewing orange blaze.

Home, we once called Earth our home.

Now, as I wake to do my round and form my message
To who knows whom, could be they are already dead
And I am like Tanya, who sang his reports
From a limitlessness so deep within the black;
To sing from this cold bridge,
His red heart must have beat like no man.

I awake from the dreamless void
Of suspended animation
With the song of Tanya in my head.
He sang,

> "I'm attracted to your tractor beam
> But you don't seem to care.
> I'm attracted to your tractor beam
> But you're dragging me no where.
>
> You've stolen all my Z's
> Turned my days into my nights
> Split my schizophrenic m-eees
> And made black holes of my lights.
>
> I'm attracted to your tractor beam
> And you don't seem to care.
> I'm attracted to your tractor beam.
> And you don't even care."

Somewhere in deep cold space
Tanya's soul floats alone
Unless he has returned before me
Listening even now for my report.

So I am alone upon the bridge.
All things hum.
The gauges read.
The fuel level's up.
Accelerating at timeless speed
The instrument is working perfectly
It's time for my report:

> Purple heather in the Hebrides,
> Blooming Lupine on a mound,
> The taste of Almond nut from the trees,
> Soil smells fresh, damp from broken ground.
>
> Once I climbed the river rock
> And shouted my name to the blue sky.
> Once, I touched a wire and got a shock
> And sunk my face into an apple pie.
>
> I ran along the beach at water's edge,
> Dove in the cool water and swam away.
> Climbed up a rock and held on a ledge,
> Sat in the sun and wasted the day.
>
> I whistled, chewed on a straw, and painted a fence;
> Swam in a wave, climbed in a cave,
> Dug in the pocket of my pants for some cents;
> Fought some boys 'cause I thought I was brave.

Now, I'm twisted as Tanya,
A singing either freak
Searching for the perfect word
Trying to make a mark with a tongue
That's frozen to the roof of my mouth,
Trying to form a sound that will be remembered
Five thousand years from now.

Coming to the realization
I can't even remember my name,
I beam my report back to command.
I miss Tanya.
I miss my mother.
What I miss most here in space
Is there is no horizon.

Poet is a Shape-shifter

Garanga, Sha-ranga, Ka-tanga-langa.
Story is the story of a big old tribe.
Ba-danga, Ba-danga, Ba-danga,
Ka-tanga-langa.
Story is the story of a big old tribe.

Garanga, Garanga,
Shifting shape moving magical cape
Sing the song and taking the shape,
Garanga, he might become Oranga Tanga.

Garanga, She-ranga, Ka-tang-a-langa,
Story is the story of a big old tribe.
Bang-a-badanga, Ba-banga, ba-danga
Ka-tanga-langa.
Story is the story of a big old tribe.

Shape shifter lifts up his wand and cry:
Words, words, now open up sky
Shape shifter dance around and jibe:
Story is the story of a big old tribe.

Ding dang dang, Organa-tang Kang
Shape shifter make the world a monkey pie.
He lift up his arms and start to fly.
Ding dang dong, he fly like bird.
He fly off on the magical word.

The Kiss

We got up before the sun.
I remember the aroma of fresh coffee.
Your hands were smooth and warm.
Even now I see the dark brown of your eyes.
The trail wound over the rocks.
Darkness. Gray clouds and dawn.
The Eastern sky exploded with orange hues.
A small bird sang crystal clear notes.
You balanced on the wood bridge.
The gate screeched open.
Granite rocks led to the ocean.
The waves smashed high white flumes.
The sand felt hot.
Cold water washed over our feet.
Your breath the ocean air.

Sunny Day Story

About Sad Silly Sue
Who wondered willy nilly
Aboard a stinky filly
Name a Nellie.

Nellie was a kind of smelly
But she knew a silly fellie
Name a Wily.

In the valley lived Wily
Which was about a miley
From where Sad Silly Sue
Wondered willy nilly
About a stinky filly
Name of Nellie.

Now shyly Wily
Was also kind a smiley
'cause he knew he had a dilly do
In Sad Silly Sue.

He wouldn't let Nellie
Wander willy nilly
Or let Sad Silly Sue
Ride a smelly Nellie.

Young Smiley Wily
Hopped upon his horsy
Name a Morsie.
Now horsy Morsie
Loved Smelly Nellie
Just like Sad Silly Sue
Loved Smiley Wyly.

Shy smiley Wily
Rode horsy Morsie
But when horsy Morsie
Saw Smelly Nellie
Horsy Morsie
Rode willy nilly.

And when shy Smiley Wily
Saw Sad Silly sue,
Shy Smiley Wily rode willy nilly too.

Begin Here

Like the bloom of a Rose when it first feels the sun
I sense a feeling inside of my heart.
As the flower that senses that now its bloom has begun
I open myself, but stop. I stop with a start.

I awake to the feeling I've been dead all my life.
That whatever I've done hasn't been right.
The order I've constructed is confusion and strife.
The sun isn't dawning. This morning's still night.

A look at the sky so full of moon
Inside I hope this feeling won't last,
Then a look at my watch. It's already noon.
I'm begging myself not to take life so fast.

I'm no longer a plant, but a tree taken root.
I can't even smile. Why I can't even frown.
I'm not even a hick. I'm some kind of coot.
Worse than a tree, I'm just an old clown.

My poetic expressions are simple statements of fear.
This is the question, for better or worse:
When it comes time to die, do I disappear?
I was last seen driving by in a hearse.

Really, the question is not: When will I die?
But since I'm always taking; When will I give?
When will I bloom, dance? When will I fly?
When at a last, when? When will I live?

Voices Behind the Mask

Masks, I hate that they are me.
These eyes that see are also mine.
My ears diseased, they can not grasp
Except a smoky wisp of sound
That can't be trapped or even viewed
Unless in afterimage like a virus
Or squiggling wiggling transparent worm
Burrowing deep with my thoughts.

These noises crave moist caves,
Hidden holes where old poems live.

Yet too loud. It's much too loud.
This din of silence drives me crazy.
Crushed stanza. Destroyed meter.
Wrecked rhythm. Ruined rime.

Old poems are vapid faces
That whisper from the musty darkness.

My lips quiver, but quiet stick,
Stuck to frozen breath that takes like metal.
Ice pick pricks, punctures my tongue.
Crushed stanza. Destroyed meter.
Wrecked rhythm. Ruined rime.

Cries and whisper reopen the wound.
And from the darkness comes the call for salt.

But I will not lend my metaphor to these rogue sounds.
Nor will I move my eyes,
Least they betray I am remembering.
I am remembering time,
A time my voice spoke singular
And what was me stood alone as icon.
Built cool from polished white marble,
Like a beacon to lost souls,
It radiated so intense, so bright,
My words had nowhere to hide,
And voices behind the mast cast no shadow.

Whispers

Cold, drizzling, and biting
This fear, the anticipation of darkness,
Nothingness,
This feeling rises like the summit.
Am I like the Tarot card, the Fool,
Stepping off the mountain's edge into space?
Am I Sisyphus pushing the rock of angst?
Will I spread my wings only to find them made of wax?

Is my immortal soul only a rime that reads
"Young, then old, then you die;
Over in the wink of an eye."

Still, the dark shadow,
The high mystery at the summit,
It tantalizes me.
I can feel the pull of its mystic talons
And hear the peel of un-struck bells.

The mountain we climb is steep and high.
It's cold and lonely and desolate.
But so far, it's been worth the climb.
My feeling is that death is a threshold
To a place for which the fresh mountain air,
Distance, space and clarity
Are only whispered metaphors.

Poet's Lament

My self is indrawn and gnarled
Retroflecting like a monster stone gargoyle
I curl into myself deeper and tighter.
Pulling and straining my ligaments
Until my muscles rupture in cramps,
Blood vessels suck at themselves,
My skin is hollow.
Eyeballs turn backwards
Trying to see if my insides are out.

Falling in nothingness.
Darkness wide and forever.
Emptiness never and never.
The landscape extends infinitely in all directions.

Beneath me flame and
A vat of boiling fire bubbles.

A seed.
A seed germinates itself.
The dried husk breaks away.
The root spreads into brown earth.
Green leaves open to the blue sky.
I sprout up with vigor.
Bright yellow sun warms me.

I bloom red, purple and gold.
Fruit hangs from my branches.

I feed the hungry.
I make shade for the weary.
I clothe the naked.
I sooth the savage.

My voice is music.
I have poetry in my soul
And prosody in my mouth.
I twice chew the stringy meat of words
Before I feed them to you.

Let them eat cake
Marie Antoinette said.
Because mares eat oaks,
And does eat oats
And little lambs eat ivy.

But poets eat the flesh of other poets.

Bright Eyes

She was a keen young thing.
And I was a toad
Laying in the middle of the road
Listening to a princess sing.

She sang, "Com Qua, Come Kee Wa,
Come down to the water with me."

"No, no," I croaked
"I'm broke," I croaked.
"I'm broke, I'm broke."

It wasn't so funny.
She was sweet, young and sunny
Rang of money,
And I could see the smoke.
But "I'm broke. I'm broke."

She sang, "Come with me Qua.
Come down to the water.
Come Qua. Come Kee Wa,
Come down to the water with me."

I'm broke.
Can't buy you honey.
Or drive my car,
Can't give you no sugar
Or light a cigar.
Can't slip off your slippers.
Or pull off your stockings.

I'm a bloke!

I'm mean, I'm broke.
I'm broke. I'm broke. I'm broke.

"Come down to the water with me.
Hop if you must. Hop till you bust.
But come Qua.
Come down, come down with me."

So what can a toad,
And a princess be told,
When you're broke . . .
Come down to the water with me.

We Becomes Us

Mixing missing hard and hollow, free being
The searing space, diaphanous, pressing
My warm belly onto yours, but where am I?
Non being, extraordinary exploded no self
The me, the mask-less mind rotating on limbic now,
Is plucked from my spin, a picked flower.
My lips press the warm flesh on your neck.
I, the eye that looked so long to see my self,
No longer looks in, but out, to the wetness of we.

Can I use the word "like"?
Like an angle? Like a shooting star?
Like a rainbow? Like a cloud?
Like the cool caress of your fingers on my lips?
Or. May I use the word "or"?
Or force my burning on your breast?
Or the thump, thump, thump of your heart?
Or is it the eternal emptiness between beats,
That freezes my frightened me, into we?

Is it alone crying, crying tears and weeping
Eyes full of distortion, mixed images,
Face contracted, palpitations, shaking,
Chin and cheeks quivering,
Guts sucked down a hollow tube,
Heart, red ripe, beating alive
Surgically laid open;
Must it be here

Alone, on the table of love,
We returns to me?

Can life go on as me, and you, and we
And not be them, they, and always thus?

In the ethereal eternal now,
In the formless forever and ever,
In our hearts, our love, our lives
With baby at your breast.

Too soon, we become us.

Cremation Ground

Come with now.
Come down.
Come with me down,
Down,
Down.
Enter the circle of prints.
Muddy foot prints run this way and that.
The ground's a chiaroscuro
Darkness, shadow, footprints, light.

Fumes of brown smoke,
Red hot flames on the horizon,
Recta-ram! Another explosion.
Or is it the sound of
Some small being, fleeting,
Burning the air,
Racing to escape the beginning
Understanding, that when it begins,
It begins to end.

Step lightly here, carefully.
You don't have to come.
Stay, don't say goodbye colored dreams.
Come with or without imagination.
Step lightly here.
Don't die. Please don't die.
The embers are our friends.

Enter the circle of rotting bodies.
If you exhale deeply
You will smell the stench
And feel the warmth.
Bend down here.
Her heart's still beating.
And see the eyes,
They're not quite fixed.
Her mouth's in the mud.
Bend down, you see. See . . .
She kisses the ground.

Ha ha ha!

She wants to live.
And she will live,
. . . in embers.
Ka Ram!
Another explosion. Bigger.

On dark horizon red flames streak upward.
In this fleeting light,
The shadows on your face,
Shrink to black tears
And drip to a dark pool.
Step in the light,
The light of embers.

Walk brightly in the circle of anticipation.
Can you taste the freshness?
Do you feel it?

Does it stop your heart?

This is the void.
The place in between,
This is pre-heaven,
Where emptiness prevails
And things aren't what they seem.
White light wails
And darkness screams
And a figure stands in an empty shroud
With one white finger exposed
To command the dying crowd.

Don't forget.
Don't forget!
He whispers.
Remember the flames.
Remember the fire.
Remember the longings and the desires,
The flames, the burning, the fires . . .
And most of all,
If . . . you can remember . . .

Remember the ember.

What I Don't Want to Hear

What I don't want to hear in a poem
Is how someone else discovered universal awareness.
How they missed love, or found love,
Or nearly discovered the truth of it all.

What I don't want to hear in a poem
Is how my little doggy Flup
Jumped in my lap
And you know what?
Then it just took a nap.

What I don't want to hear in a poem
Is some rheum nation
That turns into abomination
At the thought of how our nation
Has gone to hell and damnation.

What I don't want to hear in a poem
Is the account of strife
Words without any life
Some critical bunk
Without any spunk.

Well then,
I'd better put up,
Or shut up,
Or get shut up,
Get locked up,
In the big trunk . . .
The big old trunk
The one that holds the rest of my poetry
Which I'm now calling junk.

Reflections

Narcissus, its yellow petals cupped in bracts white
Deceives the chill and dew, the air
Until in mild fitful luster, sobs.

Cold, blue rain smeared panes collect
And like Mercury, flash.
The clouds string dark fingers
That collapse to rain.

Pride, a jealous boiling water heater,
Showers fared blaze throughout my head.
Steam furls over window cracks.
Drops bill poised.
As tears slide across my face
Like epitaphs on wet mirrored glass,
At least, I know reflections.
At least . . . reflections.

© Copyright Stephen P. Means 2012

Published by Wisdomgame®
Contact steve@wisdomgame.org
http://wisdomgame.com

Thanks for reading.

www.ingramcontent.com/pod-product-compliance
Lightning Source LLC
Chambersburg PA
CBHW071258040426
42444CB00009B/1777